Jesus pe[rformed] [many] other signs in the presence of his [disciples], which are not recorded in this [book]. But these are written that you may [believe] that Jesus is the [Christ], the [Son] [of God]. John 20:30, 31

What Do You Need?

Name _____

Circle the things you might need if you are sick.

That's Great!

Place the "great!" stickers by the great things Jesus did. Cross out the things that Jesus did not do.

Art by Len Ebert

Draw another great thing Jesus did.

What Can He Do?

Name _____

This boy is sick and must stay in bed. What can he do? Fill in the circles beside the right answers.

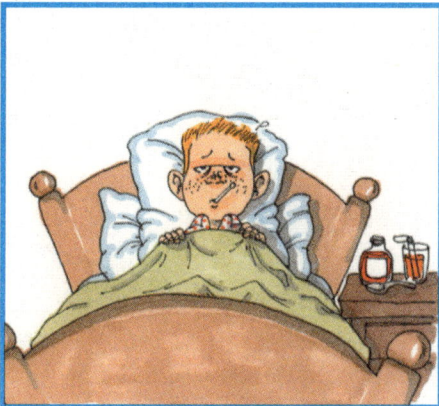

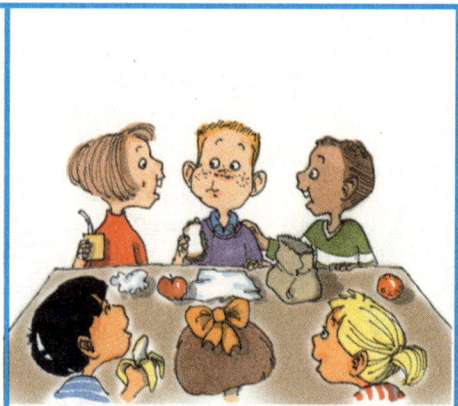

Can he go to school and eat in the cafeteria?
○ Yes
○ No

Can he read a book?
○ Yes
○ No

Can he swing?
○ Yes
○ No

Can he eat?
○ Yes
○ No

Can he play soccer?
○ Yes
○ No

Can he talk with friends?
○ Yes
○ No

Art by Christine Tripp

Ways to Tell

Discover ways to tell others that Jesus can do miracles. Write the correct word on each line or circle the correct word.

I can _____ a song about

      sing   see

Jesus' miracles.

I can _____ a picture about

      dig   draw

Jesus' miracles.

I can _____ a letter and tell

      work   write

about Jesus' miracles.

I can invite a _____ to come

      friend   flea

to Bible school with me to learn about Jesus' miracles.

Thanking Jesus

Name _____

Put the right words on the blank lines or draw lines from the words in the Word Bank to the blank lines. Discover times to thank Jesus.

Word Bank

day

hungry

thirsty

each

me

1. I can thank Jesus for [image] when

   I'm ___ ___ ___ ___ ___ ___ .

2. I can thank Jesus for my [image]

   when I get out of bed each ___ ___ ___ .

3. I can thank Jesus because He [image] ___ ___ .

4. I can thank Jesus for [image] when I'm

   ___ ___ ___ ___ ___ ___ ___ .

5. I can thank Jesus for my [image] when I get dressed

   ___ ___ ___ ___ day .

Art by Roy Green

Jesus Fed a Crowd

Fill in the circle in front of each right answer.

1

Many people followed Jesus because

○ He did miracles.

○ they did not have anything else to do.

2 Andrew found a boy with a lunch of

○ peanut butter and jelly.

○ bread and fish.

3 Jesus

○ thanked God for the food.

○ sang a song.

4

Everyone had plenty to eat. There were

○ cookies for dessert.   ○ 12 baskets of leftovers.

I Can Worship Jesus

Add the stickers to discover ways to worship Jesus. Cut on the solid lines.
Fold on the dotted lines. Glue or tape the tab under the other end.

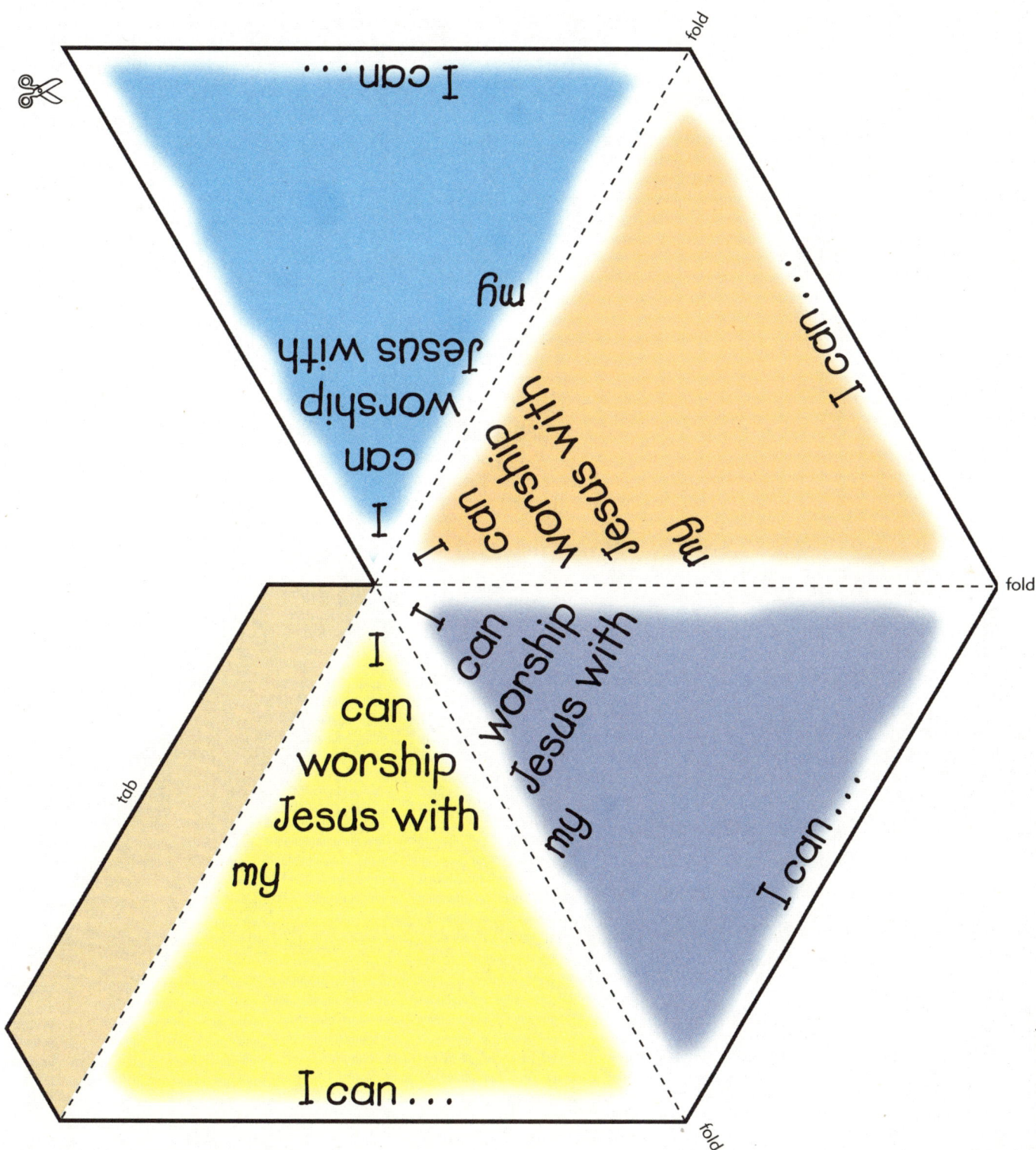

I can . . .

I can worship Jesus with my

I can worship Jesus with my

I can . . .

I can worship Jesus with my

I can worship Jesus with my

I can worship Jesus with my

I can . . .

I can . . .

tab

fold

fold

fold

Art by Michael Streff

Worship Jesus

ACROSS
3. People _____ Jesus.
5. Jesus _____ everyone.
6. After He died on the cross, Jesus rose from the _____ .

Shade one of the white shapes on the hot air balloon. Shade above that number in the roped area. When you have finished, you will know the message.

Cut apart the stickers used in different lessons. Store them in labeled envelopes until you need them.

Special Unit Bible
Memory poster

Unit 1 Bible Memory poster

Unit 1 Bible Memory poster

many   disciples   believe

book   Messiah   Son

Lesson 2

great!   great!   great!

great!   great!

Lesson 4

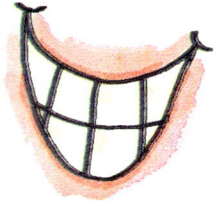   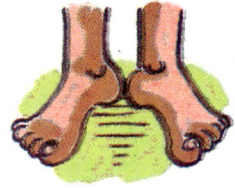

Lesson 8

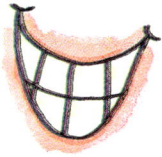  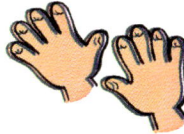  

Lesson 10

Unit 2 Bible Memory poster

Shade the cloud and field with a coin or pencil to find the Word Bank and puzzle. Use the clues and the Word Bank to help you fill in the crossword puzzle.

DOWN
1. Jesus _____ people about God.
2. Jesus _____ sick people.
4. Jesus is _____ Son.

$\overline{}_1 \ \overline{}_2 \ \overline{}_3 \ \overline{}_4 \ \overline{}_5$

$\overline{}_6 \ \overline{}_7$

$\overline{}_8 \ \overline{}_9 \ \overline{}_{10} \ \overline{}_{11} \ \overline{}_{12} \ \overline{}_{13} \ \overline{}_{14}$

Praise Jesus!

Discover ways to praise Jesus. Then draw another way to praise Jesus in the empty box.

Praise Jesus!

praise by

praise by

praise by

Jesus loves you!

praise by

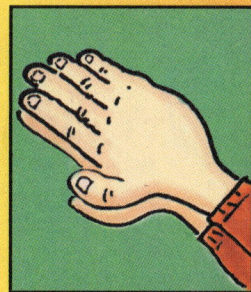

Art by Duff Orlemann

Why Worship Jesus?

Use words from the Word Bank to complete the sentences. Discover reasons to worship Jesus.

A

Jesus is

— — — — — — — — .

Jesus can do

— — — — — — — — .

M

Jesus did

— — — — — — — — — .

Jesus is

— — — — — — — .

W

Jesus

— — — — — — — —

on water.

Jesus is

— — — — — us.

H

Jesus

— — — — — — —

people.

Jesus

— — — — — — us.

Word Bank

| walked | awesome | healed | miracles |
| mighty | helps | with | anything |

What Is the Church?

Name _____

Find the following verses in a Bible. Write the missing words on the lines. Then use the Word Bank to discover some things that the church does.

Psalm 100:2   "___ ___ ___ ___ ___ ___ ___ the LORD with gladness."

The church ___ ___ ___ ___ ___ ___ ___ ___ ___ .

1 John 3:11   "We should ___ ___ ___ ___ one another."

The church ___ ___ ___ ___ ___ .

1 Thessalonians 5:17   "___ ___ ___ ___ continually."

The church ___ ___ ___ ___ ___ .

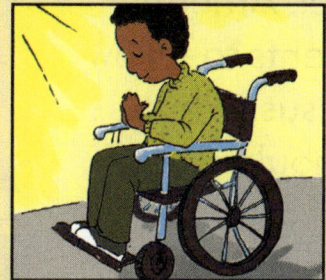

Hebrews 13:16   "And do not forget to do good and to ___ ___ ___ ___ ___ with others."

The church ___ ___ ___ ___ ___ ___ .

I'm glad you are our new neighbors.

Word Bank
loves   worships   prays   shares

Art by Duff Orlemann

Following Jesus

Draw a 🙂 by the pictures that show kids following Jesus.

Alex made fun of Evan. Evan wants to follow Jesus. What should he do?

I forgive you, Alex.

You are funny looking too, Alex.

Keisha is new at school. No one talks to her. Amanda wants to follow Jesus. What should she do?

Would you like to sit with me at lunch?

Joshua wants to play. He sees his neighbor carrying a trash can. Joshua wants to follow Jesus. What should he do?

At the Temple

Name _____

Fill in the circle in front of each correct answer.

1

A man sat by the temple gate because he could not

○ walk.   ○ hear.

2

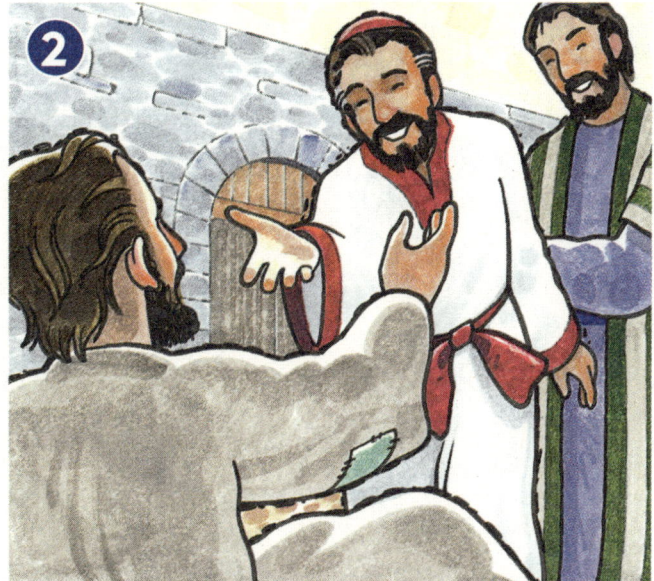

Peter told the man to get up and

○ ride a bike.   ○ walk.

3

The man stood up, walked, and

○ praised God.   ○ skipped.

4

Peter told the people about

○ Jesus.   ○ Noah.

Art by Dan Grossmann

Ways to Tell About Jesus

Add the stickers to discover ways to tell about Jesus.

1. I can use my [ ] to teach a song about Jesus to a friend.

2. I can give a [ ] about Jesus to a friend.

3. I can use my [ ] to draw a picture of Jesus to give to a friend.

4. I can invite [ ] to Sunday school, so they can learn about Jesus.

5. I can make cards to give to friends to tell them about [ ].

Puppet Fun

Draw hair on the puppet and color the face. Cut on the dotted lines. Attach both parts to a paper lunch bag. Have fun helping your puppet speak boldly about Jesus.

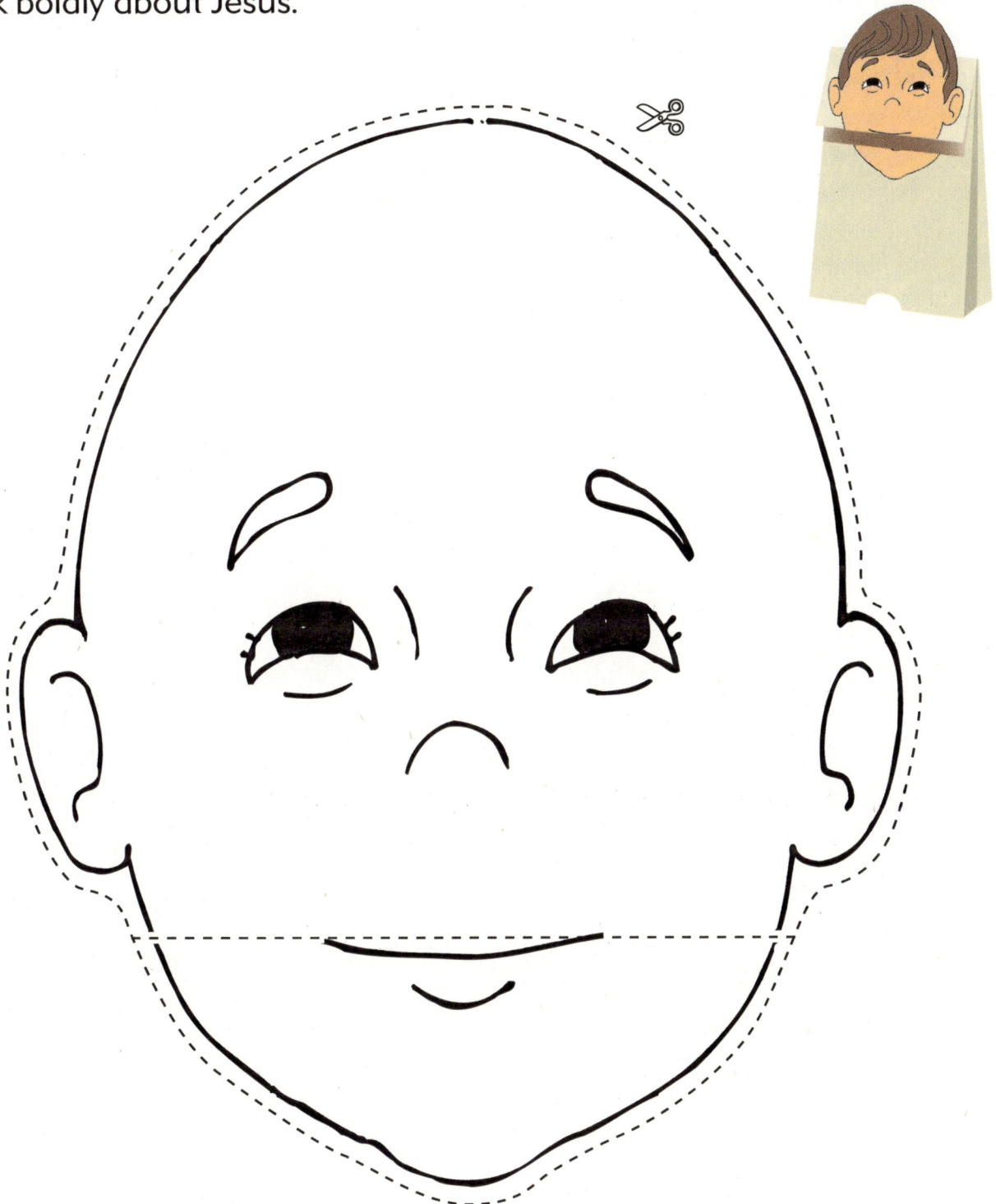

Art by Duff Orlemann

Who Said It?

Name _____

Read each sentence. Put in each box the sticker that shows who said the sentence or who spoke about someone.

1. "Do you understand what you are reading?"

2. "I need someone to explain it to me!"

3. He spoke about Jesus.

4. "Here is water. Why shouldn't I be baptized?"

Art by Len Ebert

Who or What Can Help?

Draw lines from the pictures to the Bible that shows who or what can help you understand God's Word.

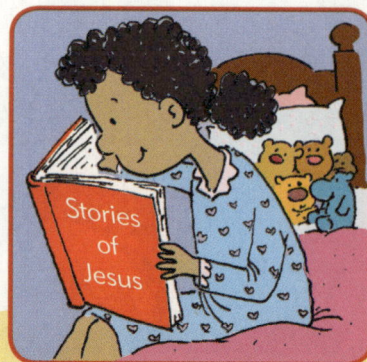

What I Believe

Cut out the title and the sentences. Make a poster using the title and the sentences that tell things you believe about Jesus.

What I Believe About Jesus

Jesus was born in a  .

Jesus was short and climbed a  .

Jesus is the Son of God.

Jesus walked on  .

Jesus made a lot of  .

Jesus did miracles.

Jesus  everyone.

Jesus died on a  .

Jesus died but came back to life.

Jesus traveled by  .

Art by Michael Streff

But Peter and John replied,

"Which is ⬆ in God's eyes: 2 ☐ 2U,

or 2 ☐ ?U be the **judges**! As ☐ us, we

cannot ☐ **speaking** about what

we have ☐ and ☐."

Acts 4:19, 20

We can . . .

follow Jesus.

Jesus loves you!

tell others about Jesus.

Jesus is alive!

speak boldly about Jesus.

Art by Duff Orlemann

Standard
PUBLISHING

www.standardpub.com

ISBN 978-0-7847-4581-6

9 780784 745816

020033313